THE STILLNESS OF THE INFINITE

18 Meditations to Deepen Spiritual Awareness through the Progressive Reflective Meditation Method

Henry Thomas Hamblin, Noel Raine, John Delafield

Hamblin Vision Publishing

Copyright

© Copyright 2024 by Hamblin Vision Publishing - all rights reserved.

The content contained within this book may not be reproduced, duplicated or transmitted without direct written permission from the author or the publisher.

Under no circumstances will any blame or legal responsibility be held against the publisher, or author, for any damages, reparation, or monetary loss due to the information contained within this book, either directly or indirectly.

Legal Notice:

This book is copyright protected. It is only for personal use. You cannot amend, distribute, sell, use, quote or paraphrase any part, or the content within this book, without the consent of the author or publisher.

Disclaimer Notice:

Please note the information contained within this document is for educational and entertainment purposes only. All effort has been executed to present accurate, up to date, reliable, complete information. No warranties of any kind are declared or implied. Readers acknowledge that the author is not engaged in the rendering of legal, financial, medical or professional advice. The content within this book has been derived from various sources. Please consult a licensed professional before attempting any techniques outlined in this book.

By reading this document, the reader agrees that under no circumstances is the author responsible for any losses, direct or indirect, that are incurred as a result of the use of the information contained within this document, including, but not limited to, errors, omissions, or inaccuracies.

CONTENTS

Concise Biography of Henry Thomas Hamblin ... VII

The Very Practical Mystic on Meditation ... XVIII

Introduction to the Meditations ... XXIV

1. Meditation 1: Good ... 1
2. Meditation 2: God as Source and Essence ... 4
3. Meditation 3: Symbols ... 6
4. Meditation 4 : Wholeness ... 9
5. Meditation 5: Oneness ... 11
6. Meditation 6: We Are One With All ... 13
7. Meditation 7: One With the Changeless One ... 15
8. Meditation 8: Surrender ... 17
9. Meditation 9: Safe Home at Last ... 20
10. Meditation 10: Absolute Justice ... 21
11. Meditation 11: Love ... 23
12. Meditation 12: Wisdom ... 26
13. Meditation 13: Beauty ... 28

14.	Meditation 14: Divine Achievement	31
15.	Meditation 15: God As Abundance	33
16.	Meditation 16: The Virtues	37
17.	Meditation 17: Divine Purity	40
18.	Meditation 18: God Transcendent	42
	About the Authors	45
	Also By	51

Concise Biography of Henry Thomas Hamblin

By John Delafield, Hamblin's grandson

Who was Henry Thomas Hamblin?

Henry Thomas Hamblin was a spiritual teacher and writer based in Sussex, England, whose message and vision were straightforward and pragmatic. He believed that the spiritual life and the practical, everyday life were inseparable. His teachings centred around the power of thought and the importance of meditation to draw on the inner power, wisdom and love that we all have deep within us. Hamblin referred to this as "the Secret Place of the Most High" in the days before the concept of meditation became well known.

Hamblin was colloquially known as HTH, and later 'The Saint of Sussex'. Whilst his teachings leaned towards esoteric Christianity, his philosophy was truly universal, embracing the truths of all faiths. The emphasis of his message is on finding the power of spirituality within us all, in the context of our everyday lives, rather than religion. As a young man, he reacted against the dogma of his strictly religious upbringing and believed that religion often divided people, while spirituality united people. His teachings came from a place of pure empathy and compassion for humankind.

Henry Thomas Hamblin worked right up to the end of his life in 1958 and left a legacy that continues to this day, its voice as much needed today as it ever was.

A Wayward Child

Henry Thomas Hamblin was born in 1873 in Walworth, South East London, of Kentish parents, and was the second of two sons. His father was very religious, and his grandfather a minister of the Baptist Church. His mother, although of diminutive size, was reportedly "great of soul" and ruled the family with benevolent autocracy. The family were poor, very poor, like all those living around them in that district of London in the late Victorian era, and, despite their hard work, the only education that could be afforded for Henry was an elementary one. He followed this with a course in technology, which proved to be of inestimable value to a youth who was considered by his parents and teachers to be wayward.

"Unstable as water; thou shall not excel," his mother reproached him regularly. No doubt she intended it to shame her son into a regime of self-improvement, in keeping with child-rearing practices of the time, but it was hardly confidence-inspiring! "Slacker!" was the repeated insult from his elder brother. Wiser, more objective, heads might have paused for long enough to recognise a certain potential in the young boy who, at the age of nine, could attempt the writing of a school newspaper. He had also established himself as something of an elocutionist. Writing and speaking would both prove very valuable skills in later life.

His adolescent years gave little indication of an error in the family verdict. "Henry the wayward" moved from one poorly paid post to another, idled in between dead-end jobs, succumbed to bouts of ill-health, and, before he had reached the age of eighteen, had displayed more than the usual "adolescent failings", according to his autobiography, The Story of My Life. From a modern perspective, all these Victorian euphemisms point to Henry being a bit of a "bad lad", and he dropped heavy hints that he had been no stranger to drinking and carousing. He suffered terribly from pangs of regret following his periods of over-indulgence, so that "Henry the sinner" became "Henry the saint" – until the next time. His pronounced rebellious streak landed him in hot water more than once. He constantly pushed against the boundaries of the fire-and-brimstone brand of Christianity in which he had been raised, which he felt to be unbearably restrictive. Reading about his struggles with authority, as a young man, somehow makes the rather aloof spiritual writer he became more accessible and endearing; it's hard not to warm to someone who so openly confesses their own faults and shortcomings, especially in the tightly buttoned-up era in which he lived. He was inspired by books, many of which fired his worldly ambition and prompted his spiritual imagination.

What his parents and educators overlooked was that Hamblin was a young man with huge aspiration, flushed with a youthful zest for life, and inspired by a worthy ambition to rise above the rut of his circumstances. Although he pushed against his father's dogmatic and punitive style of practising religion, at heart, he was deeply religious. A person's early environment, education, and adolescent behaviour can often determine the course of their life. Youthful indulgences of one sort or another are inevitable. Hamblin's studies of the New Testament, which revealed that selfishness and hypocrisy, rather than indulgence, received greater condemnation by Jesus, would have been very much in his consciousness.

A Successful Businessman

There is no doubt that Hamblin had an enquiring mind and this, coupled with a desire for scientific accuracy, enabled him to achieve success in his later endeavours in business. In this, despite his lack of education, he was bolstered by boundless faith and courage, which, coupled with a shrewd business sense, ensured that he succeeded beyond all expectation. In 1898, having taught himself opthalmics at night, he qualified as an optician and set up his first successful business as an optician, Theodore Hamblin (now Dolland and Aitchison), frequented by royalty, the rich and the famous.

Hamblin was a natural entrepreneur and a born risk-taker. By this time, he was also a family man. He married Eva Elizabeth in 1902 and they went on to have two sons and a daughter. He enjoyed acquiring several businesses, all with insufficient capital, and relying on credit and goodwill. He took more pleasure in the thrill of the challenge than in the promise of monetary gain. Far from being downcast in the face of numerous setbacks, he thrived on negotiating obstacles which appeared insurmountable. As soon as the business was established and running smoothly, however, rather than being satisfied with financial security and the ability to provide for his family, Hamblin's interest started to wane. He felt a loss of the initial drive and motivation, his physical and mental health began to decline... until the next big idea came along and away he would charge again, all fired up and raring to go.

Throughout all his wild days of youth and high-risk business ventures, Hamblin felt a great tug towards discovering a deeper meaning to life, beyond that of the daily struggle to make ends meet. Propelled by his discontent, he became a driven seeker after truth. In his quest, he met other prominent thinkers of the time and formed lasting friendships.

As his business success grew, so did a gnawing sense of depression. It was as if there was something inside him that had not yet found a voice. Around this time, he discovered the New Thought movement and began to read their publications. Hamblin realised then that none of his worldly success had made him happy. He felt that a move from London to the coast would be beneficial. Shortly afterwards came the outbreak of the First World War, and Hamblin went off to serve his country, leaving his business in the care of others, almost with a sense of gleeful relief, strange though it sounds. But it was the sudden and unexpected death of his younger son at the age of ten, in 1918, that brought him to rock bottom and to question everything.

A Very Practical Mystic

Hamblin was not a genius, and millions of other people have made good in the world with even less promising assets. But it was in the second half of his life, when Hamblin turned away from creating highly successful business enterprises to focus instead on the spiritual realm, that his unique combination of the pragmatic and the profoundly spiritual shone forth. He has sometimes been described as a very practical mystic.

Hamblin began writing in the 1920s. The words seemed to flow from him. He found that writing clarified his thoughts. One of his first books written in this new phase of his career was Within You Is The Power, which was to sell over 200,000 copies. Other books soon followed. Hamblin believed that there is a source of abundance which, when contacted, could change a person's entire life. As long as people blamed their external circumstances for any misfortune, they were stuck in the 'victim role'; but, if they moved in harmony with their inner source, their life could be full of abundance and harmony.

Soon after this, Hamblin set up a magazine called The Science of Thought Review, based on the principles of Applied Right Thinking. He wasn't discouraged by the fact that he had no experience of editing or publishing. His experience had taught him that if the mind worked in harmony with the Divine, then everything you needed flowed towards you. Anyone with any business sense at all knew that to set up a magazine with a first print run of 10,000 copies would be a risky thing to do. But Hamblin was not risk-averse, to put it mildly! He wanted to put what he believed into practice. The only magazine of its kind in the 1920s, it soon gained a worldwide readership. Among his friends and contemporaries that were to contribute to the magazine were Joel Goldsmith, Henry Victor Morgan, Graham Ikin, Clare Cameron and Derek Neville, all of them prolific and successful writers. Apart from his international subscribers, Hamblin had close ties to comparative spiritual thinkers in many other countries, especially in the US.

Although he had been brought up in a strictly religious family, he hadn't found any of the answers he sought in the Church. He realised that, rather than following any creed or dogma, which didn't work for him anyway, he had to look within himself. He found contact with 'Presence' and realised it held the key to the peace he was seeking. All the time, his search was leading him nearer to discovering the way his thoughts affected his performance and outlook.

During the General Strike of 1926, the Great Depression of 1929-32, and again in years after the end of the Second World War, many homeless, unemployed wayfarers came to the Hamblin household seeking relief and shelter. Henry and Elizabeth provided them with a simple meal, new boots and clothing and money for the road. Known colloquially as 'The Saint of Sussex", Hamblin was a man who applied his spiritual principles to his everyday life. Practical Mysticism was Hamblin's life's work. He helped people in deeply practical ways to become less fearful, happier and more successful in their lives. To this end he wrote books like The Antidote to Worry. However, later in life he realised that whilst these books genuinely helped people, they were largely concerned with the personality. He then wished to go a step further and become more fully a truly 'practical mystic', so he wrote a spiritual course of 26 lessons, each with a definite theme presented in a systematic way. This was designed to move beyond the constraints of personality so that the soul could breathe the pure air of Spirit. What was needed, he felt, was 'a total surrender of ourselves to the Divine.' The course is available as the book The Way of the Practical Mystic.

The Power of Thought

Hamblin was at the forefront of the New Thought movement which was gaining pace in the early 20th century. He discovered that 'new thought' was in fact ancient wisdom, based upon the truth that has always existed since before time began. All great souls give voice to that timeless truth in a myriad of different ways. Hamblin urges us to "Think in harmony with the Universal Mind." In other words, he underlines the fact that Truth is and cannot be changed depending upon our mood or our whim.

Hamblin realised that we need not only a positive frame of mind but an applied way of thinking - Right Thinking, as he termed it. What did he mean by that? Well, he wrote a book on it, The Little Book of Right Thinking, which is in its 17th reprint. Essentially, he defines Right Thinking as:

- Thinking from the Divine standpoint.

- Controlling the thoughts so they do not go off on negative tangents away from the Divine Truth, which is always positive.

- Replacing negative thoughts with positive thoughts

- Living in the consciousness that all is well; and as an adjunct to this, remembering that perfection exists as a reality now, and to think in the consciousness of that knowledge.

- Meditation or prayer is the highest form of Right Thinking.

- Ultimately, however, the aim is to get beyond thought, 'to enter ultimate Truth'.

He says, 'When we cease thinking, we glide out on the ocean of God's Peace. Thought brings us to the foot of the mountain after which we have to proceed by intuition'.

'Health, Wealth and Happiness. Isn't this something we all want, either for ourselves or for those dear to us? And yet, how many of us are struggling to reach or hold such a goal for a sustained period of time?'

Hamblin's teachings explain how we can achieve all of these things, not by hard work and striving but by a simple change of thought. Within You is the Power is one of his simple but profound statements, and the title of one of his books.

Hamblin was a prolific author and had many thousands of followers studying and benefiting from his teachings and courses until his death in 1958. The simple principles contained in those teachings are as relevant today as they were when he was alive, and can still help us to achieve health, prosperity and happiness if we apply them conscientiously.

He died in 1958 in Chichester Hospital. The Hamblin Trust exists to this day to propagate the legacy of his work.

The Relevance of his Teachings Today

Hamblin was, essentially, a Christian mystic, yet his ideas about the simplicity and clarity of presence seem incredibly contemporary. He believed that the source of all wisdom is within us and all around us, and that this is the fundamental reality; there is no separation, and we are all one. His message and advice to all who read his work is that it is for everyone and is in harmony with the aspiration of all good people throughout time. Hamblin believed that there can be no finite creed of an infinite faith. Moreover, he suggests that, when creeds appear, true faith can be constrained.

He cautioned that if you seek God in prayer, the corollary is that you must have faith in Him. He often stressed that no prayer goes unanswered, and, although you may not get the answer requested, your prayer will be answered in some form. God is around us and within us, and this is the fundamental reality. He made it clear that, although human organisations come and go, God's laws are eternal, and that God is the quintessence of Love, Wisdom, and Harmony. He expresses the clear view that "Blessed are they who believe and yet have not seen". The knowledge that God is born within us is fundamental to our understanding, and only by the loss of self can God be found. At the point a person surrenders his or her "self" to God, it is then that a re-birth takes place and one's real life in God begins.

Some may question this view and ask: "What is this but the core teachings of the many brands of Christianity?" In response, Hamblin's view was that modern Christianity is a heterogeneous compound of the teachings of Jesus interwoven with historic pagan-based doubts and fears, litanies, supplications and more, all of which are closely guarded by a priestly hierarchy. These were strong views, and Hamblin does not disparage those who found them uncomfortable, as he says that churches are necessary and helpful for those who are succoured by them. Hamblin had a lifelong rebellious streak where authority was concerned, and this included the strictures of the Church. Hamblin would sometimes say that the Truth of the message of Jesus was so often wrapped up in dogma and creed that its purity and simplicity were obscured.

In his teaching, he states that first comes purity of intention, reminding his readers that one cannot serve God and Mammon. Either you trust God completely or you hedge your bets by having worldly alliances and a healthy bank balance. He maintains that trying to achieve both will impair spiritual development. Secondly, an individual's dedication to following God's path will require great patience, perseverance, faith and courage; but in following this path the individual will develop forbearance and good will. He adds that other life experiences will follow naturally and lead to a developing compassion, which will enable the individual to radiate the love of God.

Where should we place Hamblin in the long line of mystics, seekers and finders? Perhaps it is rather impertinent to pose the question some 65 years after his death, but it is surely relevant to consider this point as, by any measure, he was an extraordinary person.

Remember that he was born into a life of poverty and obscurity but, despite a very limited education, by superhuman efforts of his imagination, he rose to wealth and secured an esteemed position in life, while all the time being aware of another "self" within him, a spiritual self. Dramatically, in the middle part of his life, he surrendered his material successes to follow his wider calling as a disciple of God. In this later life he did not subscribe to any specific creed or form of religion. He was no haloed saint in the traditional sense, but he would have said, "What I have done, or rather what has been done through me, can be done by any person in the world according to their gifts and personal faith".

The essence crux of this teaching is that the latent power of God lies within everyone.

The Very Practical Mystic on Meditation

by Noel Raine

There are many ways to meditate and many approaches to the subject from various schools and teachers and they all have their merits depending on the objective that meditators are seeking to achieve. Such objectives vary but, for those seeking deeper spiritual unfoldment, we are pleased to share the teachings of writer and teacher Henry Thomas Hamblin, 1873-1958.

A deeply spiritual man, he was colloquially known as *"the Saint of Sussex"* by those who were associated with him. He was described by the English nature poet, Clare Cameron, as being in the tradition of the great mystics.

His many publications and teachings on *The Science of Thought*, which he founded in 1920, have guided and inspired many thousands of people since then. Undoubtedly, Hamblin's language is a little dated now, and his writing uses religious terminology that is perhaps not so widely acceptable in our current times but was prevalent in the era in which he lived. Irrespective, the message he taught remains as true and inspiring as ever:

At the mundane level, change your thinking and you can change your life.

At the deeper level, work with the universal laws of God, or the highest spiritual energy, and your life will be transformed.

His teachings are not obscured by elaborate concepts and practices. They have one simple message – you can bring health, happiness and prosperity into your life by working with God, or whatever term one may use to describe the highest source of life energy.

That is why this short book is so exciting and why we are so pleased to be able to share it with those of you who have a desire for spiritual growth.

Hidden within the body of his book *The Way of the Practical Mystic*, which contained his course of spiritual lessons, is a series of developmental meditations. Hamblin refers to their practise as *Progressive Reflective Meditation*, an approach possibly unique to him, that provides not only a foundation for an unfolding of our spiritual understanding and development, but also a safe and gentle approach to achieving that growth.

The material included in the book *The Way of the Practical Mystic* was previously issued as individual weekly or bi-weekly lessons and was not expected to be used as simple reading matter. Mystical and spiritual growth can only develop through sincere application and inner practice and each of the meditation subjects discussed here need to be worked on inwardly over a period of time and, as Hamblin would say, through "entering the silence".

Before you start on your journey through Hamblin's Progressive Reflective Meditation, we have reproduced below extracts from some of Hamblin's books sharing his views on how best to approach the subject of meditation.

Some Thoughts on Meditation

There are many reasons why people may choose to meditate: to relax, to solve problems, to improve health, to achieve clarity of mind and so on, but Hamblin views meditation as a prelude to something much more profound, a deep spiritual objective - to become attuned to the vibrations of God, or higher consciousness, or what might be called the awakening of an inner spiritual awareness.

Hamblin's Teachings on Meditation

Hamblin's teaching is that, as a result of meditation, a higher or spiritual mind opens and begins to function – a mind which grasps deep spiritual truths without having to reason. It has direct knowledge.

When seeking divine wisdom by direct knowing, the mind must be calmed and stilled. This is done by gently yet repeatedly turning away every intruding thought until our soul is left undisturbed with God. It is then in the silence that thoughts and ideas come into consciousness, which are from God, or however we understand the highest spiritual energy.

Key Points from Hamblin's Teachings on Meditation

Thoughts

No particular posture or process is required but successful meditation depends on the ability to control the thoughts. If this does not feel possible, it is very helpful to practise a form of prayer instead, at the same time ever seeking to reach a place of stillness.

Routine

The first thing is to set aside a certain time (a few minutes at first) both night and morning, for entering the silence through meditation. The aim is to lift the heart up until a point of contact with the Divine, or the highest spiritual energy, is reached, and then rest in the "quietness". This is sometimes described as being still and knowing God.

True Silence

The term entering the silence is perhaps liable to be misunderstood. Instead of allowing ourselves to sink down into a state of passivity, we should reach up to God, or higher consciousness, until we reach a state of deep attunement and sense its spiritual power. Entering the silence is really becoming attuned to God, or our spiritual source, which means that our vibrations have to be raised to a higher pitch until they vibrate in harmony with the higher spiritual pitch or note. True silence is positive, real and substantial. Hamblin teaches that true silence is not a mere absence of noise – it is a state of alert presence or realising the presence of God. It is only in the silence that original ideas can come; ideas which often transform one's life with startling rapidity.

Technique

Hamblin's technique is not one of emptying the mind or concentrating on the breath, it is a deep focusing on a particular subject, or upon an aspect of God (or however you perceive the highest spiritual energy). This involves holding in your mind a thought of an aspect or quality of God, or the highest spiritual energy, and turning it over like a precious jewel to allow insight and illumination from higher spiritual levels to reveal to our consciousness all its various facets of truth.

Effect of Meditation on Character

The secret of meditation is that, when we meditate, what we then get to know as God, or the highest spiritual energy, becomes incorporated within our own being and character. In other words, the higher spiritual qualities which we have meditated on become reflected into our character and built into the very fibre of our being - the effect of the meditation is to change us into the likeness of that upon which we meditate.

Immersion

Ultimately, you may find that it is no longer necessary to follow any set system of meditation and contemplation – but only to know God and to feel so immersed in God's peace that you feel this peace flowing through you like a river.

This guidance has been sourced from a variety of books written by Henry Thomas Hamblin books. We hope that it will prepare you for your journey of spiritual discovery. Each of the meditations outlined here are taken from passages in *The Way of the Practical Mystic*. Each meditation is accompanied by a description of its purpose. A copy of the book *The Way of the Practical Mystic* is available for purchase from our website. www.thehamblinvision.org.uk

Finally, it is worth reiterating that spiritual growth takes time and, ultimately, becomes a life-long journey. It does not come from reading or intellectual understanding, although they can both play a part in our unfolding. The words provided in the meditations are simple and easily understood, but their worth will only be evident when they are applied conscientiously and taken to our hearts in the silence of our inner sanctums.

We hope that you will enjoy experiencing Hamblin's spiritual insight and wisdom and will benefit greatly from its application in your life.

With love and blessings from the trustees,

Noel Raine, Chair of The Hamblin Trust

Introduction to the Meditations

Going into the Silence, by Henry Thomas Hamblin

Enter the Silence both night and morning. You will possibly have difficulty in concentrating your thoughts. If so, do not say, "I cannot concentrate", or "My power of concentration is weak", for this will tend to make it worse. Rather, realize that the Infinite Mind is in you, that you are part of the Great One Mind of God. The wave is a wave and not an ocean: it has its identity and individuality, yet it is a part of the great ocean. So, also, are you part of the Universal Mind.

The realization that Love is drawing you will make it easy for you to concentrate.

The result of this method of progressive meditation is that the good effect of hours of meditation can be recalled and made use of by the uttering of a few words, or even one word, or by the thinking of one thought. Thus, in the space of, say, fifteen minutes, as much real, constructive work can be accomplished in the quiet place, as in hours of ordinary meditation.

First of all, let us review what meditation is and what it accomplishes.

Meditation is the holding in the mind of a thought of God, or aspect or quality of the Divine Character, and the turning of it over and over so as to allow the Illumination of the Spirit to reveal to our consciousness all its various facets of Truth. By our so doing, a flood of understanding comes to the soul, and new thoughts, ideas and aspects of Truth come to us. We do not discover Truth, but by turning over the thought in our mind the Light of the Spirit reveals Truth to us.

By our meditating in this way, Truth is revealed to us by inward spiritual illumination. It rushes into the soul, and we feel its power and inspiration. If, when this takes place, we quietly bask in the warmth that this inward understanding and revelation bring, just in the same way as one can bask in the rays of the sun, whatever quality of Divine Mind that we meditate upon is built into our own character. The more we bask in this manner, the more we become changed.

But there are so many things that we need: we come so far short of the Divine Character, that it would take us nearly all day to meditate upon all the qualities that we find are necessary if we are to attain to the full stature of Christ. Therefore, we must find some means whereby the process can be shortened without being impaired.

Also, to meditate in the ordinary way, at any great length, might produce mental fatigue, through having to remember all the various things upon which we have to meditate. By progressive meditation, this mental fatigue also is avoided.

When we hold a subject or idea in the upper mind, allowing the searchlight of the Spirit to play upon it, a cloud of other thoughts, ideas and meanings come flowing in, like bees attracted by a jar of syrup. Not all at once, but day by day something is added, until as a reward for patient persistence we not only know far more about the subject upon which we have been meditating, but we understand and realise and feel the wonderful inner truth which it contains. When we feel the Truth, then is the time to bask in Its rays; and the more we bask in this way, the more do we become changed into the Divine Likeness. Many students experience this feeling in the form of a warm glow. They experience a feeling of actual physical warmth which spreads outwards from the region of the heart. For my own part, I experience it in the form of a delightful feeling of rest, calm, peace and joy, sometimes accompanied by a sense of mystical light, such as cannot be described. Others have only a feeling of calm, happy conviction – and in this there is rest and peace. It does not matter which form our experience may take, it is good, and all that we need do is to bask in the feeling or realization.

It may take a long time to reach this stage of knowing: not only the weeks, or even months, spent in building up and up, until realisation comes to the soul; but also, in going over the whole ground each day.

For instance, let us take as our subject of meditation, 'All is Good'.

In order to realize this, we have to pass through a gradual unfoldment of Truth on the subject. The mind at first has to realize that there is no evil purpose in God's Scheme, and that there is only one God and one Scheme. Next, that there is no evil Principle, and that there is only one Principle and this is Good. Next, what appears to be evil may be Divine Justice in operation. Next, that apparent evil may be good in disguise. Next, that because we can know only in part, what appears to be evil may be only one side of a perfect whole. Next, that evil maybe something out of which good and order and progress are evolved, and therefore cannot be evil in actuality. And so on, almost ad infinitum. As we meditate upon the subject, fresh ideas come to us, each bringing more light and understanding. For instance, Good is omnipresent: therefore, Good is here. Good being everywhere, there can be no room for anything else; therefore, all is Good. Finally, we reach a stage of understanding, or realization, in which we know, in our very soul, that Good is the only reality, and that all evil is lack of Good, and that while it has a temporary power in this consciousness, must pass away. This understanding, or super-knowledge, brings a feeling of joy, peace or glow, as the case may be.

Having reached this stage, the work leading up to it should be repeated day by day until the feeling is always obtained, and we can bask, at will, in the warmth and sunshine of the truth that all is good.

The principal thing to be accomplished is to realize the reality and truth of Truth. Every thing already is, all that is necessary being that we should realize inwardly this great truth. The effect of true meditation is to bring Divine Light and understanding to the soul. Arguments are good, so long as such arguments are based upon Truth, that is, if they are made from the standpoint of the Universal Mind – but reflective meditation is far better. If the subject of Good is held quietly in the mind and lifted up, so to speak, to the Light of Truth, and the various aspects of the subject, as here enumerated, touched upon, then other thoughts and ideas will come direct from the Universal Mind and flood the consciousness with light and understanding.

Henry Thomas Hamblin

1

MEDITATION 1: GOOD

Gradually, through meditating quietly in the way already described, there is built up in the mind and soul a wonderful structure of Truth. If the subject of Good, omnipresent, omnipotent and all-permeating, be held continually in the mind, and also made the subject of quiet meditation, night and morning, innumerable ideas and flashes of divine illumination and understanding, together with fresh knowledge derived directly from the Universal Mind, are added to the central idea. It is like building a heavenly palace of gems and precious stones. As heavenly ideas come to the mind, they are added to the structure that is being built around the idea of Good. We do not have to do the building. Everything fits into its right place, of its own accord.

It is customary to call pleasant experiences good and those which are unpleasant, 'evil'. Yet they are both 'Good'. The human mind is so limited it can only think in pairs of opposites. On the surface, we see good and evil in conflict. We call disaster, adversity and bereavement or loss, evil, and prosperity, ease and enjoyment, good. Yet experiences teach us that the so-called good times are dangerous to our spiritual welfare, while what we miscall bad or evil times are beneficial to our soul's wellbeing. Therefore, the same experiences when looked at from a different standpoint are found to be the reverse of that which we supposed them to be; for what we called good we now call evil, while that which we called evil we now acknowledge as being good. In the lessons, also, we speak of good and evil as being relative and comparative. But this is not the Good on which we wish to meditate.

When we become further advanced in understanding, we realise that all is Good, or the offspring of Good. Sin is thinking out of harmony with Good. Sin (in essence, wrong thinking), because it separates us from Good, brings in its train every possible negative ill. Suffering, lack, ugliness, disorder, misery, disease, sickness, death. But none of these things is evil. We call them evil, but they are the highest form of good that our sin, or wrong thinking, will allow to manifest. We fear death, looking upon it as evil, but we have to confess that it is often a friend in disguise, or 'a happy release'. Whatever comes to us is Good manifesting in the only possible form that we, by our sin, wrong attitude and imperfect thinking will allow to manifest.

What, then, do I mean by Good? Good is that which transcends what we call good and evil. Good, while it may include much of that which we call evil, which, of course, is only painful or unpleasant discipline, transcends all our ideas of good and evil, and our finite way of thinking in pairs of opposites.

From this One Source, Good, the pure and perfect stream of creation and life flows. This pure stream or fountain is Infinite Wisdom and Love, flowing from the heart of God, and this is the source of all creation (as it really is). All the laws of life and the universe are based upon wisdom and love. Therefore, there is no such thing as revenge or punishment from the

Divine side. We punish ourselves, by our sin or wrong thinking, by which we separate ourselves from the Good, thus causing ourselves to suffer from every description of negative ill.

When we meditate on Good, we get beyond, or behind, what we call relative good and evil, the pairs of opposites of ordinary human thinking, the contending forces which, on the surface, produce disorder and unrest, making contact with our Divine Centre – the one pure and perfect source from which all life proceeds.

In this inner realm we find perfect peace and in place of unrest, perfect divine order instead of human disorder.

2

MEDITATION 2: GOD AS SOURCE AND ESSENCE

As we have already seen, Good may include both good and evil, or what we call good and evil. Good transcends all our finite conceptions. It is something far greater than our puny ideas on the subject of good and evil. We might argue about relative good and evil until the end of time, but we could never arrive at any understanding or clear decision. We can arrive at an interior understanding of truth only through a spiritual awakening. truth can be apprehended only by the soul, through direct knowing. No-one can explain truth, for the reason that It transcends all finite conceptions and is entirely beyond the human intellect. Whereas the finest intellect is baffled in spite of a search for truth, continued and persevered with, it may be for many years, unceasingly, the soul, through meditation, receives a flash of illumination whereby it knows the truth which forever sets us free.

The great paradox is this, that while Good may include what we term good and evil, it transcends them, at the same time excluding even the faintest idea of imperfection. All the perplexities of life and a relative universe can be solved only by meditation upon *that* which transcends them all: which is *all* and yet transcends all. The dividing line between the false teaching and the true is this: whereas the former bids men to seek after things, the latter bids them to seek the Source of all things. In our Lord's words, to seek first the Kingdom of Heaven, or God, after which all things needful are added. The Kingdom of Heaven is a state of consciousness wherein we realize our complete oneness or at-one-ment with our Divine Source. When we reach this state, or even something remotely approaching it, we realise how utterly futile is seeking for results, making demonstrations, and so on. Finding the Kingdom is so transcendent that everything else is flattened out into nothingness.

We meditate, then, upon God as the Supreme Being, Source and Essence – Good. Transcendent, beyond and above time, space and sense, behind all pairs of opposites, always beyond our highest aspirations.

Brushing aside all thoughts of time, space, conflict, opposing forces, becoming, progress, evolution, unfoldment, we direct our attention calmly and quietly upon that which was and is and ever shall be; the one eternal is-ness, who is always complete, perfect, whole and sufficient in itself.

We begin our meditation proper by thanking God that there is no change, conflicting forces, or violence, disorder or even becoming, in the secret, inner place of the Spirit, but only perfect calm, repose, divine order, and so on. While some students are capable of meditating upon abstract ideas, the majority are helped by picturing something that will act as a symbol of perfect repose, wholeness, and the stillness that is not inactivity, but is the effect of activity in perfect order, wherein is absolute poise, balance and effortless accomplishment. We shall speak more of this in our next letter.

3

MEDITATION 3: SYMBOLS

The symbols given in these letters are offered as suggestions only. For that which is beyond all pairs of opposites, and which I sometimes call the *Repose of the Infinite* (not meaning sleep, but the stillness of unimpeded activity), I sometimes use the symbol of a mental picture of a globe spinning on its axis at a speed which makes it appear motionless. Upon this globe are painted concentric circles, perhaps unevenly, yet the higher the speed the more perfect the circles appear to be. All crudeness and imperfection are 'swallowed up' by the speed at which the globe revolves. Imperfection disappears.

It is the same with our symbol. To our imagination, it presents a picture of perfect order: activity at so high a rate as to appear as stillness. No matter what disharmony we may encounter, no matter what idea of violence or disorder, one trained in meditation can lose it in the stillness.

At first, we find our symbol disturbed, to the extent that we are disturbed by what has happened or threatens to happen. When we are disturbed, the circles on our symbolic globe will not fall into their perfectly true and symmetrical form. But as we quietly meditate, denying that there can ever be any disorder of any kind in Spirit, the circles resume their perfect inherent symmetry. We then are at rest in Truth. When the circles again become true, the disorder has been overcome and we are again one with our Divine Source.

Again, I sometimes liken the perfect, reposeful, unimpeded *Activity in Stillness*, or *Harmonious Cause*, to the cosmos. The latter is, after all, a poor representation of the former, but its wonderful order and precision convey to our minds just the right idea of harmonious, effortless, reposeful precision that we need.

The cosmos, when regarded as unaffected by man's disordered thinking, presents a wonderful picture of order, calm, wholeness, completeness, balance, poise, and so on, utterly transcending all our finite ideas on the subject.

By picturing in the mind some sort of idea of the cosmos, with all the perfect working of the heavenly bodies in their passage through space, never hurried, yet never late, always in their right place, at the right time, neither one second too soon, nor one moment too late, the orderly working of the cosmos conveys to us a correct idea, although a limited one, of the one perfect causeless cause whom we adore as our divine source and centre.

We can sometimes contact *the Stillness of the Infinite* through a sublime sunset, the dawn of a perfect day, the silence of mountain peaks, the inspiration and awe of vast spaces – these may bring to us a realization of what *that* which is behind it and of which these things, lovely though they be, are only but a feeble expression.

Afterwards, by recalling whatever it was that raised the feeling, or brought realization to the soul, we can at once enter the stillness and find ourselves in the *Presence of the Most High*.

When realizing this stillness, or calm, or oneness which is behind all the change, opposition, struggle, disorder, and disunion of the surface life, we seem to enter into a larger place. Time, decay, change, death, all finite limitations, are left behind, and we know ourselves to be one with *that* which changes not.

4

MEDITATION 4 : WHOLENESS

Whatever symbol may be used, when we enter into a larger consciousness, we should remain in quiet meditation upon the symbol, breathing deeply and easily. The sense of expansion which is experienced is a form of cosmic, or universal, or super-consciousness. As we enter into the calm stillness and peace of the Infinite, our consciousness expands until it seems to embrace the whole universe.

In the Divine Presence all is good. There is nothing else but good. There is no limitation, no incompleteness, no imperfection, no disorder – only perfect wholeness.

Good therefore implies wholeness. By meditating upon the former, we are led to the latter as the next step in our progressive meditation. We therefore hold the idea of wholeness at the top of our mind, allowing the Light of Truth to shine upon it and illuminate it. As we do this from day to day and from week to week, we begin to sense, or inwardly realize, what wholeness is.

It cannot be described, simply because it is a state that transcends both the finite mind and finite language. We can, however, realize what wholeness is, in the soul. Wholeness includes completeness, perfection, order, yet seems to transcend them all.

In course of time, wholeness becomes associated in our mind with good. Ever afterwards, to think and meditate upon Good calls up a sense or realization of wholeness.

5

MEDITATION 5: ONENESS

Meditation upon wholeness brings us, in course of time, to the truth of *oneness*. The former is a transcendent truth, but the latter is, I believe, even greater.

It is impossible to describe, in finite language, the meaning of oneness. It can, however, be held in the mind, in the quiet place. Then the light of illumination of the spirit of truth, playing upon it, reveals its truth and meaning to our soul, but not to our intellect, because it transcends the human mind entirely. It can, however, be felt, or experienced, in the soul.

First is revealed to us Oneness in itself. The Oneness of the *one*, which is the Oneness of the Whole.

Next is revealed to us that we are each, individually, included in the One. This stupendous truth cannot be comprehended by the intellect but can be realized by the soul.

Knowledge of the stupendous truth of Oneness, of which we form a part, can only be felt or realized by intuition, or direct revelation. It is a spiritual experience, having nothing whatever to do with the intellect. Indeed, the more intellectual a person is, the more difficult it is for him to grasp the

Truth. It is necessary, as our Lord said, for us to lay aside our intellectual pride and become as a little child, if we are to enter the Kingdom of God.

First, then, we meditate upon God as the Supreme Good. This suggests wholeness, which, when realized in the soul, leads us on to oneness.

As we hold this idea in the higher part of the mind with the Light of Truth playing upon it, we realize that there is only the One. Stupendous and binding fact, but there it is. By meditating upon it we enter into Truth.

6

MEDITATION 6: WE ARE ONE WITH ALL

Because there is only the One, and the One is the Whole, we are included in the One.

Hold this idea in the higher part of the mind until the Light of Truth reveals its wonderful truth to you. Because there is only the One, we can never be separated from our Divine Source. The belief in separateness, ie: believing that we can ever be separated from the One, is the greatest of errors, and the sin for which we have to suffer most. When our centre is shifted and is made to coincide with the divine centre, we become one with God.

Because there is only the One and we are one with the One, we are one with all.

Hold the above in the mind, allowing the light of the spirit to play upon it until its truth is revealed to you.

Then pray:

One with the Universe. One with That which produced the Universe. One with all our fellow human beings – all one. One with every creature, both great and small.

One with the winds of heaven, and the mighty deep: the sun by day and the quiet orb by night. O Wonder of Wonders, how can I express my joy?

Because I am one with Thee, Thy Oneness is also my oneness: all sense of separateness is swallowed up in Truth.

Because I am one with Thee, Thy Completeness is also my completeness; all my incompleteness is swallowed up in Truth.

Because I am one with Thee, Thy Wholeness is also my Wholeness: all imperfection, or lack of Wholeness, is swallowed up in Truth.

7

MEDITATION 7: ONE WITH THE CHANGELESS ONE

It is necessary for us to remember that it is through Christ that we become one with God. For some reason, we are naturally fallen in consciousness from the Divine Presence, which is perfect wholeness and oneness, and it is only Christ who can raise us up to our lost estate.

Christ, the Divine One, knocks at the door of our hearts. Christianity is a 'heart' religion. We have to become as little children, 'feeling' our way, by intuition into the Kingdom, rather than 'seeing' our way by great knowledge. Christ stands at the door of our hearts and knocks for admission.

We will continue our usual meditation upon:

Good

The goodness behind all relative states and opposing forces.

Wholeness

The wholeness which includes perfection and completeness.

Oneness

The oneness which includes the Oneness of the *One*, and our at-one-ment, or oneness, with the O*ne*, and with the *Whole*.

8

MEDITATION 8: SURRENDER

Before we can come into alignment with Truth, before we can become one with our divine centre and be united with the changeless harmony and perfection, we have to surrender ourselves entirely to Christ. Our highest conception of God and truth is Christ – God made understandable to man. He is Lord of all aspiring souls. He it is who guides us and helps us by His Spirit.

But we cannot make progress, and even the Spirit cannot help us, unless we surrender ourselves, our lives, our ambitions, our wills, all to Christ. This complete surrender is the strait gate, the narrow entrance which so few find, of which our Lord speaks. "And few there be that find it".

So few are willing to make the great surrender. They are willing to enter the Kingdom by any other road than this. But they cannot, or will not, give up their self-will and personality. But there is no other entrance than this, which is by surrendering all – everything – completely to the Infinite Love.

If we do not make this surrender, we build on the sand, we erect our edifice on a false foundation, so that when days of adversity, temptation and test come, it falls to the ground in awful ruin. All teaching which leaves out the great surrender to the will of our Father in Heaven, as exhibited by Jesus in His cross and crucifixion, is false. There must be the cross, when we give up all and surrender everything, before there can be the resurrection and the new life.

Therefore, in our meditation, we adopt an attitude of complete surrender and abandonment, saying:

> *Not my will, Lord, but Thine be done. Just take me and my life and do with me and it just as Thou wilt. Bring me completely into my proper place in Thy Kingdom, the place Thou hast prepared for me. I herewith give up everything that would hinder or prevent my at-one-ment with Thee.*

This should be persevered with daily, for months, if necessary, until you are perfectly sure that a complete surrender has been made. We continue to meditate as before, especially upon our oneness with the One. The surrender not only makes this at-one-ment possible but brings it very near.

It is necessary to persevere with these (or similar) words of surrender. We may think that we have surrendered ourselves entirely to Infinite Love (Christ), but we find that we still cling to self and to the things that chain us to the lower life. We have to be uprooted, out of the old soil of sin, vainglory, selfishness and pride, before we can be replanted in the garden of the Lord. First one branch is severed from the earth and then another, and as each comes away, we think that we are entirely free; but we find that what has come away is only one of many root branches, that there are many others.

We need patience and perseverance in surrender. It is useless and foolish to rush on before we have become liberated entirely from the old life, the old desires and the old self-will. But when we have become entirely separated from the old life, and liberated altogether from self-will and separateness, the master plants us in His own garden of love.

9

MEDITATION 9: SAFE HOME AT LAST

And so, having made the great surrender, we come to the quiet place, where God abides, and find ourselves home at last. The strife and the battle over, the tempestuous voyage at an end: *Safe Home at Last.*

We thank Thee, Father, because we, who were once afar off, have been brought near by the blood of Christ. It is only such love as this that could have broken our hearts, won our wills, reconciled us to Thee, and brought us into Thy Kingdom. We thank Thee that In Christ we are forever One with Thee. We, the willing 'victims' of Infinite Love, now meditate upon this truth.

Brought home.
At one, forever one.
No parting,
No more separateness,
Forever one
In Christ
With Thee
And God wipes tears from off all faces.

10

MEDITATION 10: ABSOLUTE JUSTICE

We meditate as before, realizing our at-one-ment with God, in Christ.

One with Thee, the Infinite Good.
One with Thee, the Infinite Wholeness.
One with Thee, the One.
There is only the One, and I am one with Thee.

Now I thank Thee that Thou art the principle of absolute justice. The scales of justice are delicately and accurately balanced. I am at the point of balance, swinging neither up nor down, neither to the right nor to the left – one with Thee.

Identified with Thee, perfect principle of absolute justice.

Because I am one with Thee, the principle of absolute justice dominates my life, and regulates my thoughts and actions, so that integrity, probity, righteousness, straightness, squareness, honesty of thought and purpose are expressed in all that I do.

When this meditation has been thoroughly absorbed, Good will always be associated in consciousness with absolute justice, with which we are one. Justice, absolute and complete, becomes part of our life.

11

MEDITATION 11: LOVE

We now meditate upon God as *Love*. We have not done so before, for it was necessary to establish in our minds the truth that God is good, is one, is whole, is justice. The majority of us - in a sickly, sentimental sort of way – have some idea of the Deity being love, but very imperfect idea of God as justice. Both are intertwined and mingled together. Indeed, they are one. Love is not perfect if it is not allied with Justice.

So now we meditate upon God as *Love*.

Love draws us to our divine centre: wisdom guides us. Love is integrating. It holds the universe together. If we obey Its dictates, we become drawn to the heart of God.

It is only Love that can 'soften' us and make us pliable or plastic enough to be recast in the divine mould, refashioned in the divine likeness, becoming completely at one with the *one*.

By obeying love's call, by surrendering to its claims, by obeying its laws, we enter into the Kingdom of Heaven. The Lord of Love takes us and plants us in His garden of love.

'Behold, what manner of love the Father hath bestowed upon us, that we should be called the sons of God!'.

So through Love we become sons of God.

When once by meditation the truth of God as love has become absorbed into our very being, then ever afterwards meditating upon God as good and the one with whom we are one will call up this truth of God's love.

Already, if we have mastered what has been taught in these letters, meditating upon our oneness with the One will call up to our unconscious mind the truth that God is good, the truth that God is wholeness, the truth that God is one, the truth that God is justice. Now we add to it: *God is love.*

Slowly, we are building up our beautiful palace of truth.

When starting our meditation at this stage it is necessary for us to touch briefly upon the various points which we have mastered.

> *God as Good, beyond all pairs of opposites.*
> *God as Wholeness.*
> *God as One.*
> *Surrender to the One.*
> *God as Justice.*

What has been learnt and realized by the soul through meditation upon these aspects of Truth will be recalled at once and flood the consciousness.

Later, they will all be recalled automatically as soon as we turn to God and meditate upon Him and our oneness with Him.

12

MEDITATION 12: WISDOM

In course of time, by simply meditating upon our oneness with the One we are put 'in contact' with all the divine ideas, or qualities, upon which we have previously meditated, so that everything that we need is poured into us, as we quietly rest in the truth of our at-one-ment with our Divine Source.

We will now meditate upon *Wisdom*.

Love and wisdom form the stem of the Divine Logos, our Father-Mother God, Father, love – Mother, wisdom. Love is the masculine aspect of God, wisdom, the feminine.

We reflect upon wisdom that is infinite. Only wisdom that is infinite could have planned this universe, foreseen all, and arranged for everything to happen just in the right way and at the right moment, in spite of man's freewill.

We worship and adore the wisdom that makes no mistakes, encounters no difficulties, and which has foreseen every problem with which we are faced, or may be faced, and provided a way of escape.

We cannot, however, with our finite minds, understand or grasp what Infinite Wisdom means. Therefore, we hold the thought or idea of Infinite Wisdom at the top of our mind, keeping all other thoughts away from it, thus allowing the light of the spirit of truth to beat upon it, to bring illumination and understanding to the soul.

When we have mediated some time in this way, with the idea of Divine Wisdom in our mind for the spirit to illumine, we can say:

Infinite Wisdom is now guiding in all my affairs; therefore all my decisions are wise decisions, and I am led to do just the right thing at the right moment, so that the whole of my work and activities is brought into harmony with the divine will and purpose, thus allowing the divine order to manifest itself, without effort and without strain.

13

MEDITATION 13: BEAUTY

The secret of meditation is this, that when we meditate, what we know God to be becomes incorporated with our own being and character. That is to say, the qualities which we have associated with God, and, through meditation, have realized to be part of God's being and character, become reflected into our character and built into the very fibre of our being.

For instance, if, in our past meditations, we have realized God as wholeness, health, completeness, etc (which allows no room for disease, sickness, or any other lack of wholeness), directly we turn to God and meditate upon Him, realizing His presence and our oneness with Him (the *One*), our consciousness becomes built up by, or impregnated with, a sense, or understanding of wholeness, health, completeness, and so on. What I want you to understand is that although we may not meditate upon God as wholeness, health, etc., but only bask in His presence, the healing process takes place.

In the same way, whatever other qualities we have associated with God, such as Oneness, Unity, Good, Love, Wisdom, Justice, and so on, become reflected into our character, being and consciousness, whenever we meditate upon God.

Thus our work in meditation, if well and soundly performed, is constructive and cumulative. First, we lay the foundation, next, the ground floor, and after that, the superstructure. Our meditation is not something that has to be done all over again every day. We do not have to begin at the foundation again and again, but at where we left off. The foundation must, however, be well and truly laid. There is nothing to be gained and everything to be lost by attempting to go ahead too quickly, thus scamping the work.

We turn now from the ugliness and squalor of life, as man has made it, and meditate upon *Beauty*.

Divine Beauty: The Beauty Inherent

The reality is infinite beauty. God is not a being of ugliness or imperfection, but of beauty beyond our wildest flights of imagination.

Recall the most glorious picture of beauty that Nature has ever presented to your view, and it will lead your thoughts and imagination to some conception of the inherent beauty of God. If I had the pen of a ready writer and the tongue of an angel I might describe, in a feeble measure, something of the Beauty of God, or of God as Beauty. But whatever I might write or say would convey but little to your soul. The only way to realize God as Beauty is to hold the Idea of Beauty in the top of your mind then think of the most beautiful manifestation of God that you can recall, and meditate upon it, allowing the Spirit of Truth, Who alone can help us to realize the Truth, to lead us higher and higher, until we realize God as Beauty.

You will not be able to describe that which you realize, but you, yourself, will know.

There must be, of course, an entire absence of strain, anxiety and effort. We have to rest quietly, with our mind raised to the divine object of our meditation, allowing the spirit of truth to bring understanding to our soul, and light to our consciousness.

'In quietness and confidence' is the great secret.

This aspect of divine mind should be meditated upon daily until it is thoroughly mastered, so that immediately you commence meditating upon God as beauty you enter into a realization of this facet of Truth.

But God is beyond beauty, or any other attribute.

14

MEDITATION 14: DIVINE ACHIEVEMENT

There is no true success apart from Thee. Thou art the only success, and we can be successful only as we ally ourselves with Thee. Therefore, we meditate upon: *Divine Achievement.*

By allying ourselves with God, and by identifying ourselves with the inherent success of the Divine Mind, we make possible the only true success. True success is not ruthless, made at the expense of other people. God does not succeed at the expense of anyone, but only by helping them and loving them. In the same way, we become successful by loving and serving others.

We identify ourselves with the One Who never becomes tired, and Who never gives up.

We identify ourselves with the One who keeps on until everything is accomplished and all things are brought to pass.

We identify ourselves with the strong and patient One – the One who changes not.

Through identifying ourselves with the Infinite One, our minds become expanded and capable of receiving larger ideas which come to us direct from then Universal Mind.

Through identifying ourselves with the Infinite One, the One Who knows no failure and can meet with no opposition or difficulty, our success becomes already accomplished. We have only to keep on, be patient, and never give up.

Having reached the right attitude of mind, we sit restfully in the Silence, with the thought of God's success and divine achievement held quietly in the top of our mind.

15

Meditation 15: God As Abundance

Failure is often due to an inclination to stand still, to be satisfied with present achievement, and to a desire to retire and take things easily.

This is against the law of life, which is growth, expansion and progression. We must go on growing like a plant, we must expand, and become bigger, so that we can fill higher and more responsible positions and do larger and better work.

Instead of retiring from our difficulties we must work through them and find liberty on the other side. The new life is a mounting upwards, always, to higher and better and more glorious things.

So we come again to the quiet place and meditate calmly and peacefully upon God as *Abundance*.

A Prayer:

> *We meditate not upon transient material wealth but upon Thee, the one unchanging Source of all things.*

God, the One, Unchanging, Unfailing Source of all things, we meditate upon Thee.

Thou canst never fail, Heaven and earth may pass away, but Thou are the same eternal Unfailing Source of Supply.

We brush everything else on one side and recognize our unity with Thee: the Centre, the Source, the Fountain of Inexhaustible Supply.

Because we are in a state of oneness with Thee, Who art unchanging, we can never be moved.

Because we are in unity with Thee Who can never lack anything, we also can never lack.

Because we are eternally in Thy care, all our needs are abundantly met.

We envy no-one their wealth, but we desire that all may know Thee Who art the Centre and Source of all true wealth, for Thou art the one and only Substance. with Thy children, therefore we desire to hold, or possess, nothing, but simply to use Thy riches in Thy service, for the extension of Thy Kingdom.

There is a point in consciousness which, in course of time, we discover; or which is revealed to us, through patient practice of meditation. This is the Inner Holy of Holies, the Heart of God, the Centre of the Universe, the Fount from which all manifestation springs. This Point, or Centre, is changeless and eternal. It transcends all pairs of opposites: it is deathless and disease-less: It is unaffected by change and decay: It is the very Life of Life Itself.

By entering into unity with this Centre, with the thought of Abundant Supply in our mind, a God-sense of wholeness, as related to supply, in which there is neither lack nor limitation, is added to our consciousness. When we become God-conscious of abundance, we think as God thinks on this matter, so that poverty can never have any place in our life.

So we come to this secret, holy spot, making contact with this inner Centre of centres, with the thought of *God as Man's Abundant Supply* in our mind. Keeping our mind fixed on this point of contact, we say: "Thou art in me, my Source of Abundant Supply".

Now "rest in the Lord". Keep in contact with your centre and keep also the sentence just given, in the top of your mind, and remain so for several minutes. Those who find supply a difficulty should meditate in this way for about twenty minutes a day always. It is their chief problem, and through overcoming it by meditation they will find the Kingdom of God.

It is useless to do this mediation for a time and then get slack and neglect it. It is useless to follow it by fits and starts. It must be done perseveringly and persistently, always. When, however, the trouble has been completely overcome so that prosperity and abundance become a habit, or automatic, this meditation can be added to those previously given, so as to form part of the mosaic which is being gradually built up.

Then, whenever we meditate upon the One, and our oneness with this Divine Centre, of which we have been speaking, abundance as well as health, wholeness, wisdom, love and so on, will be unconsciously meditated upon, much to our present well-being and eternal welfare.

16

MEDITATION 16: THE VIRTUES

By this time, you will see that by meditating upon all the qualities and excellencies of the Divine Character we build up a series of contact points between ourselves and the Eternal Father (and Mother) Spirit. Through this cumulative meditation our unconscious mind is taught to know God as One, Good, Wholeness, Health, Love, Wisdom, Justice, and so on. A soon as we meditate upon God and our oneness with the Divine Source, through all these points of contact, or recognition, Divine Life flows into us, building us up in the very qualities which we have associated with God, in our progressive meditation. We thus make use of the well-known mental law of association.

Several of the most important 'points of contact' have been given you, but it will be unnecessary to give all of the remainder in detail, for you have only to apply the teaching you have already received to the following (and also others that may occur to you) in a progressive manner in order to continue the 'building'.

It must be pointed out, however, that each quality must be meditated upon day after day, and week after week, and, if necessary, month after month until it is mastered and becomes built firmly into the consciousness. Jerry-building is worse than useless.

Also, about once a week you should refresh the memory of your unconscious by meditating briefly upon each of the main qualities upon which you have meditated in the past. This need not take very long but should be done deliberately. All attempts at haste are fatal and defeat the object in view. As each quality is touched on, realization and understanding should come quickly, almost at once. Then, after you have rested in the realization for five seconds or so, the next quality should be dealt with in the same way.

Now the remaining subjects for meditation are these: knowledge, endurance, fortitude, long suffering, meekness, temperance (moderation, restraint), charity, joy, peace, compassion, humility, diligence and purity.

There is therefore work for years to come in meditating upon these spiritual qualities as parts of God's character, so as to make them form part of our own.

After our meditation upon a new aspect or quality of Divine Character, we should realize and affirm our oneness with the One, so that the quality becomes ours, not by nature, but by participation, through Grace.

In order to help you to refresh the unconscious memory by going over the ground which has already been covered, the following brief resumé is given. It may be read over quietly and slowly, each 'point of contact' being meditated upon for a few seconds in turn.

'I worship and meditate upon Thee, O Infinite Being, Who art infinite Good,

'Transcending all pairs of opposites, all relative states and conditions:

'Who art also One.

'I thank Thee because as there is only the One, I am included in the One, therefore, I am in Thee through Christ.Lord of Love, and in Him become one with thee, forever.

'I thank Thee also that Thou art infinite:

'Justice,

'Love,

'Wisdom,

'Beauty,

'Achievement,

'Supply,

'Because of my oneness with Thee, through Christ, all these things find expression through me'.

Now meditate solely upon God, basking in the Light of His Presence.

17

MEDITATION 17: DIVINE PURITY

We have already used *Love* as our meditation, and also a list has been given you of other qualities which we have to meditate in order to make our meditation complete. At the end of this list is Purity. This is, however, of such importance that it must be treated separately.

No-one should go ahead too quickly and attempt too much. The great life-force cannot be transmuted all at once, but only by degrees. If we become gradually emancipated that is all that the Spirit expects of us.

Now I am quite sure of this that the object desired cannot be attained by fighting against our natural feelings and desires, or by looking upon them as evil; but only by meditating upon *Divine Purity*.

By thinking of chastity and continence and so on, we produce in the mind a feeling of repression. "Thou shalt not" is the idea generated. By meditating, however, upon *Purity* there is no repression: there is no idea of crushing out or smothering anything: there is perfect freedom and harmony – but on a higher plane.

Through meditating upon Purity, we become changed. Old harmful repressions are dissolved away: lower desires are transmuted: certain emotions are transformed into pure, universal love.

Just what Purity is cannot be described; it is something far more transcendently beautiful than we can imagine, but Divine Mind knows our desire to be cleansed of all that belongs to the lower nature, from all love that is selfish. And the Holy Spirit, whose glorious function it is to pray for us, pleads for us in yearnings that can find no words, interprets our desires aright, so that our prayer, or meditation, is in harmony within the Divine Will. Through this 'intercession', or Divine prayer, on our behalf, we become changed into the image of that which we desire. In other words, we grow into the likeness of our Lord.

So then, we hold the thought of Purity in the top part of our mind and just rest in the Divine Presence with our face turned towards the Light, with this idea uppermost. As we do this the dross and earthly desires are purged away, the lower is transmuted into the Higher, and we become changed from glory unto glory.

18

MEDITATION 18: GOD TRANSCENDENT

After each statement of Truth, pause and realize the truth of the Truth. Where possible visualise what you are saying. Where actual visualising is not possible, endeavour to feel the reality of the Truth.

There is no evil – in thee, or life's purpose: there is only infinite good.
Thou art the infinite good, there is nothing beside thee.
Thou art the infinite perfection: thou art all there is.
Thou art the infinite loveliness and beauty: the infinite brightness, glory and radiance.
Thou art the infinite love: the infinite kind purpose.
Thou art the infinite joy and peace, the quiet haven of all weary souls.
Thou art the rock of ages, where all who trust thee can hide in the storms of life.
Thou art the eternal, changeless, infinite, glorious reality.
All the cosmic fellowship of saints adore thee.
Thou art the infinite abundance and supply: the inexhaustible wealth and profusion.

Thou art the infinite success, accomplishment and achievement.
Thou art the infinite perseverance, persistence, overcoming and victory.
Thou art man's perfect guide in life, leading him every step of the way.
Thou art the infinite wisdom.
Thou art the infinite knowledge.
Thou art the infinite understanding.
Thou art the absolute truth.
Thou art the infinite justice, integrity, uprightness, probity.
Thou art the infinite life and health, wholeness and completeness.
Thou art the infinite protection and care.
Those who place their trust in thee can never be betrayed.

Remember that the object of all this is simply to find the Secret Place of the Most High and to enter into its peace, and a realization that all is well, and that we are rooted in God and established in Eternal Life. This is the great 'treatment': to know God and to abide in His Truth. This brings about a Divine adjustment of the whole life. When we reach this consciousness, we are aware that all good is attracted to us, and is coming to us, and that all we need is already ours, because we have entered the Stream of our true destiny.

Established in the Infinite, realizing your Eternal Nature, standing firm on the Rock, Christ, nothing can disturb you. As an eternal being, you are a Centre through which Divine Power flows, and a magnet drawing to yourself all necessary good.

*"All the Divine Forces minister to you...
the winds are your messengers over all
the world,
and flames of fires your servants to fulfil
your will,
to fulfil your eternal joy".*

About the Authors

HENRY THOMAS HAMBLIN, NOEL RAINE, JOHN DELAFIELD

Henry Thomas Hamblin

Henry Thomas Hamblin (1873-1958), author of the best-selling titles *Within You is the Power* and *The Power of Thought*, was one of the founders of the New Thought movement early this century. Although a Christian mystic himself, he believed that too often religion divided people, while spirituality and truth united people. For this reason, he embraced and was tolerant of all religions. The late Swami Dass of India referred to him as 'the Saint of Sussex' after visiting Mr HT Hamblin in England.

Noel Raine

Noel Raine is the Chair of the Hamblin Trust. A retired accountant, Noel divides his free time between his work for the Hamblin Trust and the Rosicrucian Order.

John Delafield

John Delafield is a former Royal Air Force pilot, retiring with the rank of Air Commodore, and eight-times National Gliding Champion. He is the grandson of Henry Thomas Hamblin; esoteric, Christian mystic, spiritual teacher and prolific writer.

Born in 1938, in the last days of peace before the world was plunged into the dark years of the Second World War, John spent his earliest years living with his grandparents, Eva Elizabeth and Henry Thomas Hamblin, at their home in Bosham near Chichester, on the south coast of England. War caused much disruption in his family, as in so many others. His father served at sea with the Royal Navy and his mother was largely absent. His childhood recollections are principally of his time with his grandparents, who were his anchor in his early years.

Although John did not take much interest in spiritual matters as a youngster, he quietly absorbed much of the wisdom of the teachings, which formed a powerful backdrop to his life. The influence of both of grandparents on his life has been profound. In his retirement, he is dedicating himself to propagating the timeless wisdom of his grandfather's teachings by revising them for a modern readership.

Also by John Delafield

Gliding Competitively (A& C Black)

A Flying Life (Mereo Books)

The Remarkable Life of Henry Thomas Hamblin, Mystic and Successful Businessman (Mereo Books)

Available at Amazon and major book retailers

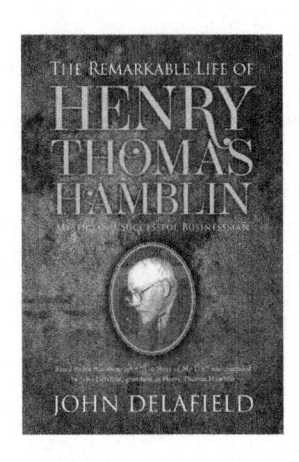

A Note from John Delafield:

The life experience of my grandfather, Henry Thomas Hamblin, often known as HTH, and the philosophy he developed, was principally of the omnipresence of God with a clear focus on the teachings of Jesus Christ. Although he had a broad appreciation of the power of other beliefs to help a searcher find God, he wrote that God was latent within every human being. In today's language he might have said that every human is 'hard-wired' to need God but that this feature must be activated. He would certainly say that God is with us now and always.

He believed that health, happiness and a sense of achievement are the normal state for mankind but that to achieve this state the individual needed to align with what he referred to as 'Cosmic Law' which he also referred to as The Truth. Over his 45 years as a prolific author, the emphasis of Hamblin's work developed from suggesting to his readers how to change their lives through 'right thought' and faith to teaching them how to find a living consciousness of God within themselves. It was this process which led him to publishing a monthly magazine called The Science of Thought Review which endured for some 85 years before being re-orientated as a larger sized printed magazine entitled New Vision (later to be called Hamblin Vision) which endured for a further 20 years and is now on-line only. Hamblin's work continues to this day through the Hamblin Trust, which propagates the work he began in 1921, when he was in his mid-40s, and, in keeping with the times of 100 years later, now operates in an online environment, publishing some of his books as well as Hamblin Vision, the magazine that follows the path established by the original The Science of Thought Review.

This project was undertaken in commemoration of a century of my grandfather's wisdom shining a light in the world.

Thank you for purchasing this book. If you have enjoyed reading it, please consider leaving a review. It takes just a moment, and helps small publishers like us boost the visibility of our books, so that other readers can find our titles. Thank you – your time is much appreciated.

You can scan this QR code by holding your phone's camera to the code. A prompt will appear, which will take you directly to the 'leave a review' page.

To review in the US, please scan the QR code below or follow this link: https://amzn.to/3WUN29c

To review in the UK please scan the QR code or follow this link: https://amzn.to/3SWomMx

Also By

Henry Thomas Hamblin

Divine Adjustment

God Our Centre and Source

God's Sustaining Grace

Life Without Strain

My Search for Truth

Power to Transform the Life

Simple Talks on the Science of Thought

Some Thoughts on Thought

The Antidote for Worry

The Life of the Spirit

The Little Book of Right Thinking

The Message of a Flower

The Open Door

The Path of Victory

The Power of Thought

The Psychology of Prayer

The Shrine of Love

The Story of My Life

The Way of the Practical Mystic

Within You is the Power

Pamphlets and Booklets

Daily Meditations

God, The Infinite Good

God's Sustaining Grace *(20 meditations on Divine Care)*

His Wisdom Guiding *(A book of daily readings from HTH's writings, compiled by Clare Cameron)*

Not an Easy Life but a Victorious One *(Reprint of Science of Thought Article)*

Release From Fear *(A practical manual on overcoming fear)*

Simple Talks on Science of Thought *(A series of 12 small pamphlets)*

The "Power Series" (Four booklets of 24/30 pages: Power to be Well, Power to Overcome, Power to Succeed, Power to Transform The Life)

The Fundamentals of True success

The Lord is My Shepherd (A study of Psalm XXIII for the practice of Affirmative Prayer)

The Lord's Prayer (An Interpretation)

The Way of Escape (An attempt to put Truth into a simple form for beginners)

Printed in Great Britain
by Amazon